Our Hardship

Joni Eareckson Tada

ROSE PUBLISHING/ASPIRE PRESS

Torrance, California

God's Hand in Our Hardship
© Copyright 2014 Joni Eareckson Tada

Aspire Press, an imprint
of Rose Publishing, Inc.
4733 Torrance Blvd., #259
Torrance, California 90503 USA
www.rose-publishing.com
www.aspirepress.com

All rights reserved. No part of this publication may be reproduced, stored in a retrieval system, posted on the Internet, or transmitted in any form or by any means without the prior written permission of the publisher. The only exception is brief quotations in printed reviews.

All Scripture quotations, unless otherwise indicated, are taken from the Holy Bible, New International Version®. NIV®. Copyright © 1973, 1978, 1984 by International Bible Society. Used by permission of Zondervan. All rights reserved.

Printed by Regent Publishing Services Ltd.
Printed in China
December 2013, 1st printing

Contents

Understanding God's
Role in Our Suffering 5

Tough Questions, Honest Answers.............11

  1. If God hates suffering, why doesn't
    he get rid of suffering in the world? 11

  2. Why do honest, good people have to
    suffer so? Don't they deserve better? 14

  3. What possible good can come through
    suffering that is out of our control?...................18

  4. Is Satan responsible for suffering? 21

Suffering and Healing 25

What the Bible Says about
God's Sovereignty 27

Does God Need Forgiveness? 42

The Author

Joni Eareckson Tada, the founder and chief executive officer of Joni and Friends International Disability Center, is an international advocate for people with disabilities. A diving accident in 1967 left Joni Eareckson, then 17, a quadriplegic in a wheelchair. After two years of rehabilitation, she emerged with new skills and a fresh determination to help others in similar situations. She founded Joni and Friends in 1979 to provide Christ-centered programs to special needs families, as well as training to churches. Through the organization's *Christian Institute on Disability*, Joni and her team have helped develop disability ministry courses of study in major Christian universities and seminaries. Visit us at www.joniandfriends.org.

Understanding God's Role in Our Suffering

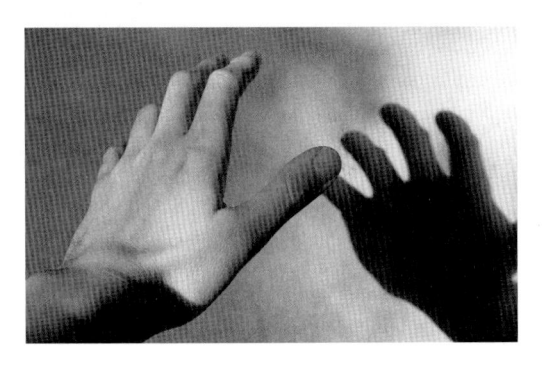

Everyone who takes the Bible seriously agrees that God hates suffering. When he walked on earth, Jesus spent much of his time relieving suffering. And we are to do the same—the Bible tells us to feed the hungry, clothe the poor, visit prisoners, and speak up for the helpless. When we feel compassion for people in distress, we know that God felt it first. He shows this every day, even now, by raising sick people from their beds, often to the wonder of doctors. Every day God grants childless couples babies, pulls depressed people out of the pits, protects those with Alzheimer's from crossing the street, and writes happy endings to sad situations. Even when he has to punish sin, he says in Ezekiel 18:32 that it gives him no pleasure.

All of creation waits eagerly for Christ's return when sin, sorrow, and suffering will be done away with (Isa. 35:5–6, 10; Rom. 8:22–23). But until the kingdom of God comes in fullness to earth, sin, sorrow, and suffering simply come with being human. Thankfully, though, God loves to redeem our sin and our suffering, as well—all for our good and his glory!

A personal perspective from Joni

The Lord took absolutely no pleasure in my broken neck. Like any father who has compassion on his children, God grieved to see me hurt. Yet at the same time, it pleased the Lord to permit my accident. My spinal cord injury was his sovereign design for my benefit and for his good pleasure.

How can this be? God's ways are so much higher than ours. I once heard Dr. John Piper say that God has the capacity to look at the world through two lenses—through a narrow lens *and* a wide-angle one. When God looks at a painful event through a narrow lens, he sees the tragedy for the hurt it is. He is deeply grieved. God feels the sting when a child dies of cancer or a husband is killed in an accident. However, when God looks at that same event through his wide-angle lens, he sees the tragedy in relation to everything leading up to it as well as flowing out from it. He sees a mosaic stretching into eternity—it is this mosaic with all its parts that brings him delight.

When I was first injured, I was desperate to understand this. That's when my friend Steve Estes showed me Lamentations 3:32–33, "Though he brings grief, he will show compassion, so great is his unfailing love. For he does not willingly bring affliction or grief to the children of men." In the span of a single verse, the Bible asserts that the Lord brings grief, yet he does not *willingly* bring grief. True, God allowed my accident to happen, but he didn't get a kick out of it—it gave him no joy. God tried this out on himself. He willed the death of his own Son, but he took no delight in it. God saw how Jesus' death would demonstrate his incomprehensible mercy, as well as bring his people to glory. God often wills what he despises because—and only because—he has a wide-angle view on the world. As Steve once told me, "God permits what he hates, to accomplish that which he loves."

How can a good and loving God allow suffering?

The core of God's plan is to rescue us from sin. Our pain and poverty and broken hearts are merely symptoms of the real problem. God cares most not about making us comfortable, but about teaching us to hate our transgressions and to grow up spiritually to love him. In other words, as we head for heaven, God lets us continue to feel much of sin's sting through our suffering. This constantly reminds us of what we are being delivered from, exposing sin for the poison it is. Thus, one form of evil (suffering) is turned on its head to defeat another form of evil (that is, our transgressions), all to the praise of God's wisdom.

Tough Questions, Honest Answers

1. If God hates suffering, why doesn't he get rid of suffering in the world?

If God were to eradicate suffering from the world, he would have to get rid of sinners—suffering is inextricably linked to our rebellion against God back in the garden. But God does not want to obliterate sinners; he wants to save them. John 3:16–19 reveals God's heart about saving sinners. When the kingdom of heaven came to earth with the arrival of Jesus, God opened the way for unbelievers to be rescued through Christ's death. If at that point God had ushered in the fullness of the kingdom and closed the curtain on suffering (doing away with all pain and heartache), what would have become of us? We wouldn't have been born, let alone had a chance to embrace Christ!

God is rich in mercy toward us! He is delaying closing the curtain on sin and suffering so that more people—millions more over the last 2,000 years—might come to know Christ. Until Jesus returns, our sufferings drive us to reach out to unbelievers with the good news: God so loved the world that he gave his only begotten Son for their salvation. The cost of suffering may be great, but people are worth it.

> For God so loved the world that he gave his one and only Son, that whoever believes in him shall not perish but have eternal life. For God did not send his Son into the world to condemn the world, but to save the world through him. Whoever believes in him is not

condemned, but whoever does not believe stands condemned already because he has not believed in the name of God's one and only Son (John 3:16–18).

🍓 The LORD is not slow in keeping his promise, as some understand slowness. He is patient with you, not wanting anyone to perish, but everyone to come to repentance (2 Pet. 3:9).

> If you believed the eternal state of your neighbors and unsaved family members was worth the suffering you face in this world, how might that change things?

2. Why do honest, good people have to suffer so? Don't they deserve better?

This world is *full* of pain. We look at the anguish that good friends are experiencing and insist, "Good people deserve *better*." But do we? It's a tough question, and the Bible has a hard answer. It paints a sobering picture: people are *not* innately good. It also says that people—all of us—cannot begin to comprehend how our sin has offended God. In fact, the Bible states that God is just and right to send rebellious creatures to hell— dare we say that he is fair to give us a "taste" of what that hell might look or feel like through our sufferings here on earth?

But wait! There is a hidden mercy here! By tasting suffering in *this* life—hell's splash-over—people are driven to ponder what may face them in the next life. In this way, suffering may be our greatest mercy. If we experienced nothing but ease and comfort, we would soon forget that we are eternal creatures—but suffering won't allow that. It persistently reminds us that something immense and cosmic is at stake: a heaven to be reached for Christ's sake, and a hell to be avoided.

Every day of our short life has eternal consequences for good or ill. Thus, it is only fitting that a merciful and wise God should give us some sense of the stakes involved, some sense of the magnitude of the spiritual battle—he does this by giving us foretastes of heaven in the joys we experience, and foretastes of hell in our suffering.

> All of us have become like one who is unclean, and all our righteous acts are like filthy rags;

we all shrivel up like a leaf, and like the wind our sins sweep us away (Isa. 64:6).

- The heart is deceitful above all things and beyond cure. Who can understand it? (Jer. 17:9).

- What shall we conclude then? Are we any better? Not at all! We have already made the charge that Jews and Gentiles alike are all under sin. As it is written: "There is no one righteous, not even one; there is no one who understands, no one who seeks God. All have turned away, they have together become worthless" (Rom. 3:9–12).

Philippians 1:27 says to "conduct yourselves in a manner *worthy of the gospel of Christ.*" We tend to look at our own conduct as the standard of virtue (measuring our Christ-likeness by our own good behavior). And so, we end up judging ourselves *by* ourselves, making a whole list of virtues our own when, in fact, the Bible says we are to conduct ourselves in a manner worthy of *the gospel.*
Read James 1:23. What does it mean to look in the mirror of God's law? When you do... what do you see?

3. What possible good can come through suffering that is out of our control?

It's one thing to muster a submissive attitude toward God when we bring troubles on ourselves, but it's a different matter when unexpected trials hit us broadside—trials not of our own making. Like when a drunk driver veers across the yellow line. Or a grim-faced doctor diagnoses cancer. Or reassessment slaps your property with a higher tax burden. Or a clumsy linebacker breaks your high-school kid's leg in football practice. Or an old friend drags your name through the mud. You didn't bring any of these troubles on yourself; these are circumstances over which you have no control—and for that reason, they're the hardest with which to deal.

But look at the apostle Paul. He didn't bring that shipwreck on himself. He didn't instigate a death threat in Damascus. He didn't orchestrate mob scenes that left him smashed by stones. Paul may not have been responsible for his circumstances, but he *was* responsible for the way he reacted.

He never groaned, "Oh, for Pete's sake, here we go again!" Instead, he said, "For Christ's sake, I delight in hardships." Another response? He said in 2 Timothy 2:10, "Therefore I endure everything for the sake of the elect..." These were the first words out of Paul's mouth when he was pelted by stones, sidetracked by brutal floggings, and thrown into dark dungeons. He endured hardships for Christ's sake, as well as the sake of the church.

- That is why, for Christ's sake, I delight in weaknesses, in insults, in hardships, in persecutions, in difficulties. For when I am weak, then I am strong (2 Cor. 12:10).

- You intended to harm me, but God intended it for good to accomplish what is now being done, the saving of many lives (Gen. 50:20).

> **Q** When suffering that is out of your control wreaks havoc, what is your first reaction? Why do you think we look for someone to "blame"?

4. Is Satan responsible for suffering?

Yes, Satan *is* responsible—imagine a ship called *Evil* that Satan fuels with his wicked schemes (and all the suffering that accompanies it). Satan may stoke the belly of that ship, but God sovereignly intervenes and "steers" that ship to accomplish his own plans and purposes. God is the "stowaway" on Satan's ship, erecting invisible fences around Satan's fury and bringing ultimate good out of the devil's wickedness. So God's decrees allow for suffering to happen, but God doesn't "do" it.

These are deep waters: God permitting suffering but not necessarily "doing" it? How does he pull it off? Welcome to the world of finite humans trying to comprehend an infinite God. What is clear is that God permits all sorts of things he doesn't approve of. He allows others to do what he would never do—take the sufferings that fell upon Job, for instance: God didn't steal Job's camels or entice the Chaldeans to wreak havoc, yet the Lord did not take his hand off the wheel for a nanosecond.

Restraining grace

Sometimes in Scripture, it's hard to tell exactly who is behind all the heartache and hardship, and we wonder, *are Satan and the Lord in cahoots with one another?* Take the following verses:

- But this time also Pharaoh hardened his heart... (Ex. 8:32).

- But the Lord hardened Pharaoh's heart... (Ex. 10:20).

So which is it? Who did the hardening of Pharaoh's heart? When it comes to Pharaoh's stony resolve and exactly *who* did the hardening, Scripture points to both Pharaoh and the Lord. We know from James 1:13 that God does not inject the idea of evil into anyone's heart. So how is it that "the LORD hardened Pharaoh's heart"?

Through the common work of grace in our world, God is constantly staving off evil, restraining the fury of Satan so that harm and calamity do not overwhelm us. The devil can only do what God allows. Every once in a while, however—as in the case of Pharaoh— God lifts his hand of restraining grace to allow evil men to carry out their wicked plans, *only as it serves God's higher purposes.* God was inasmuch saying to Pharaoh, "So you want to sin? Well, go ahead, but I'll make sure that when you do, your evil intentions suit *my* higher purposes and plan."

Even though humans have intellects and wills of their own, God ultimately governs all they do, including the results of their evil intentions. And he does it *all* without impugning his righteous and holy character.

Suffering and Healing

It is true that disease flows from Adam's rebellion and God's curse; it is part of the "wages of sin" caused by our fall. It is also true that Jesus came to reverse that curse. But does this mean Christians shouldn't have to put up with cancer, Down syndrome, Lyme disease, or Alzheimer's? Isaiah 53:5 says, "He was pierced for our transgressions, he was crushed for our iniquities; the punishment that brought us peace was upon him, and by his wounds we are healed."

We'd like to think that since Jesus came to take up our diseases, there should now be *carte blanche* healing for everything from migraines to menopausal sweats. But that's like saying: "There's an oak in every acorn—so take this acorn and start sawing planks for picnic tables." Or it's like saying, "Congress just passed a Clean Water Act, so tomorrow morning Manhattan residents can start drinking from the East River." Forty years will pass before that oak is ready for lumbering. Purging industrial ooze out of a river will take decades. And so it is with Jesus' reversal of sin's curse (and the suffering that goes with it). What Jesus began doing to sin and its results won't be complete until Jesus comes again. The *purchase* of salvation was complete and the outcome was settled with certainty. But the *application* of salvation to God's people was anything but finished. God *has* saved us, yet we are still "being saved" (1 Cor. 1:18). We are still on earth—this means we're still going to feel the influence of that old curse. At least until heaven!

What the Bible Says about God's Sovereignty

All Christians acknowledge that God holds ultimate power in the universe. But does he always *exercise* it, especially when humans suffer? The causes behind human suffering are listed as major categories below. Under each are Scriptures asserting God's *active* (not merely reactive) control.

God exercises control over the forces of nature

- **Exodus 9:23, 26** When Moses stretched out his staff toward the sky, the LORD sent thunder and hail, and lightning flashed down to the ground. So the LORD rained hail on the land of Egypt.... The only place it did not hail was the land of Goshen, where the Israelites were.

- **Psalms 147:12, 15–18** Extol the LORD, O Jerusalem; praise your God, O Zion... He sends his command to the earth; his word runs swiftly. He spreads the snow like wool and scatters the frost like ashes. He hurls down his hail like pebbles. Who can withstand his icy blast? He sends his word and melts them; he stirs up his breezes, and the waters flow.

🌿 Mark 4:36–41 Leaving the crowd behind, they took him along, just as he was, in the boat. There were also other boats with him. A furious squall came up, and the waves broke over the boat, so that it was nearly swamped.... He got up, rebuked the wind and said to the waves, "Quiet! Be still!" Then the wind died down and it was completely calm. He said to his disciples, "Why are you so afraid? Do you still have no faith?" They were terrified and asked each other, "Who is this? Even the wind and the waves obey him!"

God rules over the animal world (including disease-causing microorganisms)

- **Exodus 8:21, 24, 30–31** "If you do not let my people go, I will send swarms of flies on you..." And the Lord did this. Dense swarms of flies poured into Pharaoh's palace and into the houses of his officials, and throughout Egypt the land was ruined by the flies.... Then Moses left Pharaoh and prayed to the Lord, and the Lord did what Moses asked: The flies left Pharaoh and his officials and his people; not a fly remained.

- **Numbers 22:28** Then the Lord opened the donkey's mouth, and she said to Balaam, "What have I done to you to make you beat me these three times?"

- **1 Kings 17:2–4** Then the word of the Lord came to Elijah: "Leave here, turn eastward and hide in the Kerith Ravine, east of the Jordan. You will drink from the brook, and I have ordered the ravens to feed you there."

- **Matthew 17:27** [Jesus speaking to Peter] "But so that we may not offend them, go to the lake and throw out your line. Take the first fish you catch; open its mouth and you will find a four-drachma coin. Take it and give it to them for my tax and yours."

God exercises control over tools and technology

- **Exodus 14:24–25** During the last watch of the night the Lord looked down from the pillar of fire and cloud at the Egyptian army and threw it into confusion. He made the wheels of their chariots come off so that they had difficulty driving. And the Egyptians said, "Let's get away from the Israelites! The Lord is fighting for them against Egypt."

- **Proverbs 16:33** The lot is cast into the lap, but its every decision is from the Lord.

- **Daniel 3:27–28** [Setting: Shadrach, Meshach, and Abednego are thrown into a blazing furnace by King Nebuchadnezzar for refusing to bow down to a golden image. The soldiers who throw them in are burned, but the three are unharmed. Amazed, the king calls for them to come out.] The satraps, prefects, governors and royal advisers crowded around them. They saw that the fire had not harmed their bodies, nor was a hair of their heads singed; their robes were not scorched, and there was no smell of fire on them. Then Nebuchadnezzar said, "Praise be to the God of Shadrach, Meshach and Abednego, who has sent his angel and rescued his servants!"

God rules over the thoughts and actions of humans

The Bible clearly teaches that God governs even human beings, who have intelligence and wills of their own.

- **Proverbs 16:9** In his heart a man plans his course, but the LORD determines his steps.

- **Proverbs 19:21** Many are the plans in a man's heart, but it is the LORD's purpose that prevails.

- **Proverbs 21:1** The king's heart is in the hand of the LORD; he directs it like a watercourse wherever he pleases.

Most Christians willingly acknowledge God as the ultimate source of all people's good deeds.

- **Ezra 1:1** In the first year of Cyrus king of Persia, in order to fulfill the word of the Lord spoken by Jeremiah, the Lord moved the heart of Cyrus king of Persia to make a proclamation throughout his realm and to put it in writing: [The Jewish exiles may return to Israel.]

- **Acts 16:14** One of those listening was a woman named Lydia, a dealer in purple cloth from the city of Thyatira, who was a worshiper of God. The Lord opened her heart to respond to Paul's message.

- **Romans 7:18** I know that nothing good lives in me, that is, in my sinful nature. For I have the desire to do what is good, but I cannot carry it out. [The point: Human nature, left to itself, never chooses the truly good; it chooses good only when aided by God.]

- **2 Corinthians 8:16** I thank God, who put into the heart of Titus the same concern I have for you.

But the Bible is equally clear that even people's wicked, deluded actions are under God's rule. He is not the source of their wicked deeds, for James 1:13 says that God tempts no one. Rather, he sees to it that people give expression to their own sinful desires in such a way as to fulfill his plans unwittingly, not their own. He accomplishes this by infinite wisdom beyond our grasp.

- **Genesis 45:7–8** [Joseph, to his brothers who sold him into slavery.] "But God sent me ahead of you to preserve for you a remnant on earth and to save your lives by a great deliverance. So then, it was not you who sent me here, but God. He made me father to Pharaoh, lord of his entire household and ruler of all Egypt."

- **Deuteronomy 2:30** But Sihon king of Heshbon refused to let us pass through. For the Lord your God had made his spirit stubborn and his heart obstinate in order to give him into your hands...

- **Psalm 105:25** Whose [Egyptians] hearts he turned to hate his people...

- **Acts 4:27–28** [The early Christians are addressing God.] Indeed Herod and Pontius Pilate met together with the Gentiles and the people of Israel in this city to conspire against your holy servant Jesus, whom you anointed. They did what your power and will had decided beforehand should happen.

Even Satan and demons must bow to God's authority

- **Job 2:4–6** Satan replied ... "Stretch out your hand and strike his flesh and bones, and he will surely curse you to your face." The Lord said to Satan, "Very well, then, he is in your hands; but you must spare his life." [The point: Satan knew he could not touch Job without God decreeing it: "Put forth Thy hand."

God assigns the harassing of Job to Satan, yet clearly defines the limits beyond which he cannot operate: "Very well, then, he is in your hands; but you must spare his life."]

- Matthew 4:10–11 Jesus said to him, "Away from me, Satan! ... " Then the devil left him....

- Luke 22:31 Simon, Simon, Satan has asked to sift you as wheat... [The point: Satan would not ask for permission if the power was already his, for it is not his nature to limit his actions simply to avoid displeasing God.]

In summary, all beings, things, and actions fall under God's rule

- Exodus 4:11 The LORD said to him, "Who gave man his mouth? Who makes him deaf or mute? Who gives him sight or makes him blind? Is it not I, the Lord?"

- Psalm 33:10–11 The Lord foils the plans of the nations; he thwarts the purposes of the peoples. But the plans of the Lord stand firm forever, the purposes of his heart through all generations.

- Lamentations 3:38 Is it not from the mouth of the Most High that both calamities and good things come?

- Isaiah 45:7 I form the light and create darkness, I bring prosperity and create disaster; I, the Lord, do all these things.

- Ephesians 1:11 In him we were also chosen, having been predestined according to the plan of him who works out everything in conformity with the purpose of his will.

🐛 **1 Thessalonians 3:3** You know quite well that we were destined for [trials].

It's clear from these Scriptures and many more that God decrees all things, even to the point of allowing human suffering, but Satan often is the messenger of those decrees even as he fights against the God who issued them. When Satan, evil people, or "accidents" bring trials upon us, we can answer with Joseph to his brothers who sold him into slavery, "You intended to harm me, but God intended it for good" (Gen. 50:20).

Does God Need Forgiveness?

With so much suffering, *some* Christians say we ought to forgive God—not just for earthquakes and tsunamis that wipe out whole villages, but for small afflictions, too. When people go through deep pain or hurt, or an abusive situation at home, some counselors advise that in order for emotional healing to take place, one must first forgive God for allowing the abuse to happen.

This happened to Roy, an elderly man struggling with the last stages of macular degeneration. His city is buying up the property his house is built on, and he may lose his home. He's also losing his son-in-law to cancer. Although a Christian, Roy is confused. Some people have counseled him, "Roy, you need to forgive God for all this!" *Forgive God?* Don't those counselors have it backward?

The Bible never directs us to do such a thing. To "forgive" God implies that he has done something wrong. But has he?

Job lost everything he had in one day—his flocks and herds, his working animals, his servants, and finally even his children. When he got all the bad news, "Job got up and tore his robe and shaved his head. Then he fell to the ground in worship... In all this, *Job did not sin by charging God with wrongdoing*" [italics mine] (Job 1:20–22).

The Bible says that nothing—not cancer, blindness, or eviction from our homes, not even abuse from others—*nothing* can separate us from the *love* of God (Rom. 8:35). So are we to forgive God for loving us too hard? Our human inclination may want to charge God with wrongdoing, but God's dealings with us are always motivated by love and concern for our souls.

So what *is* the right thing to do? Hebrews 12:3 tells us, "Consider him who endured such opposition from sinful men, so that you will not grow weary and lose heart." Look at the way Jesus forgave and even loved those who nailed him to a tree—consider afresh the enormous sacrifice Jesus made. No matter how much we are suffering, it's good to focus on what Jesus did for us at Calvary. "For the message of the cross is … the power of God" (1 Cor. 1:18). If we want to understand God's hand in our hardship—as well as experience God's power in that hardship—all questions are put to rest at the Cross!

> Amy Carmichael once said that we should never forget that the *way* of the Cross *leads* to the Cross; it doesn't lead to a bank of flowers. Miss Carmichael said that if we're looking for a bank of flowers, then we know nothing of Calvary's love.

Good can come through suffering

- Suffering can cultivate a proper reverence and respect for God in our hearts.

- It helps us appreciate the sacrifice Christ made to rescue us from hell.

- It fills our hearts with gratitude to Jesus who bore our sins and who will ultimately put an end one day to sin, suffering, and sorrow.

- Suffering can remind us of God's patience and loving kindness toward an unbelieving world. It is only by the restraining hand of God that the world has not disappeared with a fiery roar.

- Suffering pushes us to let go of the sins that Christ suffered to forgive.

- Suffering is the textbook that teaches us about our true selves and what is hidden in our hearts.

- Suffering reminds us that this life can never keep its promises, and it lifts our sights toward heaven where one day every tear will be forgotten.

- Affliction unites us with Christ as we share in the fellowship of his sufferings.

- Hardships increase our empathy toward others who face similar problems.

Books by Joni Eareckson Tada

The topics of fear and hopelessness, depression and suffering, loneliness and worry are issues that author Joni Eareckson Tada can speak to personally. Let Joni tell you her secrets to peace and joy. She knows that God does not take pleasure in seeing you suffer. He has compassion for you and gives you many ways to deal with life's pain so that you can have peace.

Making Sense of Suffering

When you're overwhelmed by pain and problems, it's easy to feel helpless, hopeless, and sinking into a whirlpool of self-pity. Joni Eareckson Tada knows about these emotions first hand. Joni shares biblical insights that bring hope and comfort to those who are trying to make sense of their suffering.

Paperback, 4"x 6", 48 pages, ISBN 9781628620467

God's Hand in Our Hardship

When you read through the Bible, you can see that God hates suffering. So why doesn't our all-powerful God get rid of suffering? Joni Eareckson Tada tackles the big questions about suffering: How can a gracious and loving God allow anyone to suffer? Why do "good" people have to suffer? What possible good can come through suffering?

Paperback, 4"x 6", 48 pages, ISBN 9781628620474

Breaking the Bonds of Fear

Is fear causing you to lose sleep, stress out, and worry? When Joni Eareckson Tada experienced a tragic accident that left her quadriplegic, fear gripped her life. Joni explains the steps she took—and still takes daily—to grow in confidence in the Lord and break the bonds of fear.

Paperback, 4"x 6", 48 pages, ISBN 9781628620481

Prayer: Speaking God's Language

How can we draw closer to God in prayer? How can we "speak God's language"? As Christians grow in the discipline of praying, it becomes clear that there is always more to learn. Joni Eareckson Tada shares personal stories and insights that will help you hone your skill of praying with the Word of God.

Paperback, 4"x 6", 48 pages, ISBN 9781628620498

Available at www.aspirepress.com or wherever good Christian books are sold.